Items should be
shown below. I
borrowers may
telephone. To renew, please quote the number on the
barcode label. To renew online a PIN is required.
This can be requested at your local library.
Renew online @ **www.dublincitypubliclibraries.ie**
Fines charged for overdue items will include postage
incurred in recovery. Damage to or loss of items will
be charged to the borrower.

**Leabharlanna Poiblí Chathair Bhaile Átha Cliath
Dublin City Public Libraries**

Dublin City
Baile Átha Cliath

Terenure Branch Tel: 4907035

TICA

dson

ork • Minneapolis

Date Due	Date Due	Date Due
7/2		
18/5	07. DEC. 13.	
05. JUN 09	-6 MAR 2015	
15/12/09		
03. 01. 12		
14/3/13		

This book was first published in the United States of America in 2005.
First published in the United Kingdom in 2008 by
Lerner Books,
Dalton House,
60 Windsor Avenue,
London SW19 2RR

Website address: www.lernerbooks.co.uk

This edition was updated and edited for UK publication by Discovery Books Ltd., Unit 3, 37 Watling Street, Leintwardine, Shropshire SY7 0LW

Words in **bold type** are explained in a glossary on page 30.

British Library Cataloguing in Publication Data

Donaldson, Madeline
   Antarctica. - (Pull ahead books. Continents)
   1. Antarctica - Juvenile literature 2. Antarctica -
   Pictorial works - Juvenile literature
   I. Title
   998.9

   ISBN-13: 978 1 58013 335 7

Photographs are used with the permission of: © Kevin Schafer, pp. 3, 9, 15, 16-17, 19, 25; © Paul Souders/WorldFoto, p. 6; © Keith Robinson/B&C Alexander, p. 7; © Josh Landis/National Science Foundation, pp. 8, 24, 26-27; © Royalty-Free/CORBIS, p. 10; © Tim Davis/CORBIS, p. 11; © Gerald and Buff Corsi/Focus on Nature, Inc., pp. 12, 14, 18, 20; © Paul Drummond/B&C Alexander, p.13; © F. Todd/B&C Alexander, p.21; © Michele Burgess, p. 22; © Eugene Schulz, p. 23. Maps on pp. 4-5 and 29 by Laura Westlund.

Printed in China

Whee! Where could you watch
penguins slide across thick ice?

The **continent** of Antarctica!
A continent is a big piece of land.
There are seven continents on Earth.

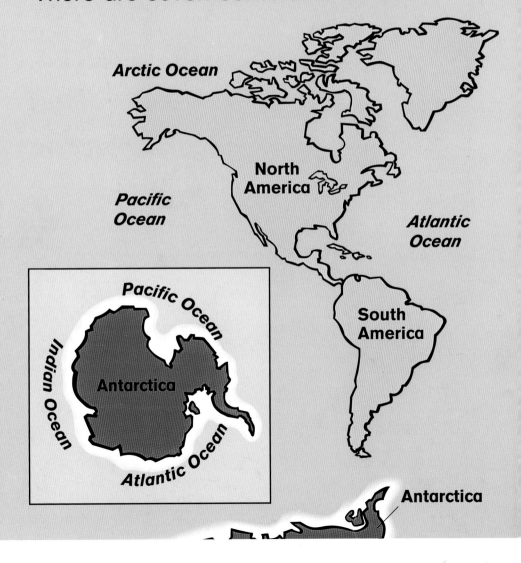

Arctic Ocean

North America

Pacific Ocean

Atlantic Ocean

Pacific Ocean

Indian Ocean

Antarctica

Atlantic Ocean

South America

Antarctica

You can find Antarctica on a **globe.**
Antarctica is at the bottom. Oceans
surround Antarctica.

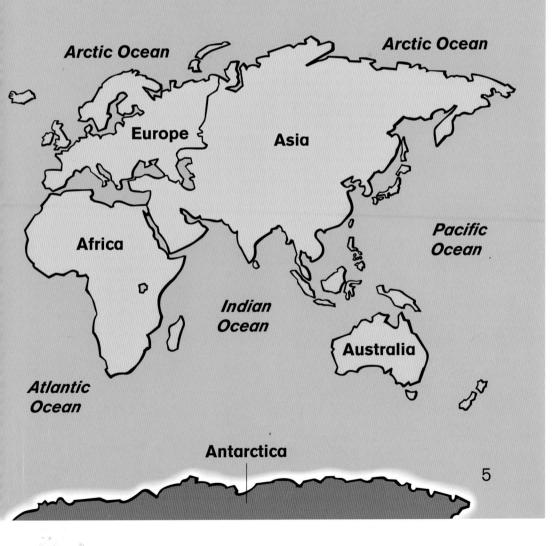

Arctic Ocean

Arctic Ocean

Europe

Asia

Pacific
Ocean

Africa

Indian
Ocean

Australia

Atlantic
Ocean

Antarctica

Deep ice and snow cover Antarctica all year round.

Plop, crash! Sometimes a large piece of ice breaks off from Antarctica. The chunks of floating ice are called **icebergs.**

The Transantarctic Mountains cross
the whole continent. They are covered
in thick ice that never goes away.

This very old ice sometimes looks blue.

Antarctica is the coldest place on Earth. Strong winds blow through Antarctica.

Brrrr! Sometimes the winds blow hard.
Then Antarctica feels even colder.

Not many plants and animals can live in Antarctica. It is too cold.

But this bird, called a sheathbill, can live there.

Seven different kinds of penguins make their homes in Antarctica and on nearby **islands.** These are gentoo penguins.

Chinstrap penguins look like they have a strap under their chins.

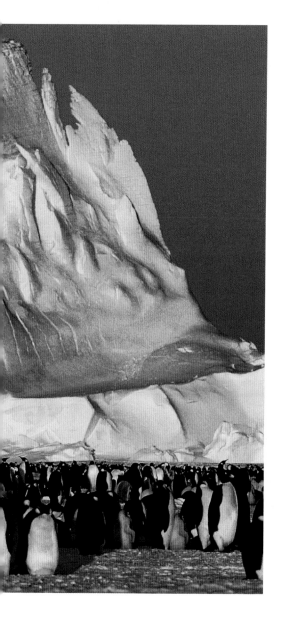

Groups of emperor penguins huddle together. They are warming baby penguins, called **chicks.**

Penguins swim in the cold ocean.
They catch fish for food.

The penguins' wings work like flippers.
The flippers help penguins swim fast.

Seals sleep all day long. They keep warm by staying close to one another.

Whales visit Antarctica's waters
in the summer.

This ship is bringing people to visit Antarctica. But no one lives there all the time.

Many **countries** send **scientists** to study Antarctica.

The scientists study the air, the ice and the wildlife of Antarctica.

Other people come to Antarctica just
for fun. They must dress warmly.

Do you know about the South Pole?
The South Pole is at the very bottom of
the Earth.

Explorers have travelled there by
dog sled, by plane and on skis.